RONALDO

To the Top!

2011	On February 14, officially announces his retirement from football.
2009	Wins the Copa do Brasil (Brazilian Cup) with Corinthians.
2008	Another knee injury ends his contract with Milan. Begins playing for Corinthians.
2007	Begins playing for AC Milan.
2006	Scores three times during the World Cup finals in Germany, becoming the top scorer in World Cup history with 15 goals in four tournaments.
2003	Begins playing for the Spanish club Real Madrid, and wins the scoring title and the Spanish League championship.
2002	Is top scorer as the Brazilian team wins the Korea-Japan World Cup. Chosen as best player in the world by FIFA for the third time.
2000	On April 5, his first son, Ronald, is born. A second serious knee injury keeps him off the field for 15 months.
1999	Wins second Copa América title with the national team. Marries Milene Domingues. Suffers his first serious knee injury while playing for Inter Milan.
1998	Suffers an epiletic attack hours before the World Cup final; Brazil is runner-up to France in the World Cup.
1997	Moves to Inter Milan, which he helps to win the UEFA Cup. Brazil wins the Confederations Cup Elected best player in the world by FIFA for the second time.
1996	Etarts to wear the shirt of the Spanish club FC Barcelona. Elected for the first time the best player in the world by FIFA. Earns the nickname "Phenomenon" Helps the Brazilian national team win the Copa América.
1995	Becomes the top scorer of the Dutch League and wins the Dutch Cup with PSV Eindhoven.
1994	Earns his first cap for the Brazilian national team that would win the country's fourth World Cup title in the United States. While in reserve, he became a world champion at age 17.
1993	Signs first professional contract with Cruzeiro.
1976	Ronaldo Luiz Nazário de Lima is born on September 22 in Rio de Janeiro.

© 2013 by Mason Crest, an imprint of National Highlights, Inc.

ISBN-13: 978-1-4222-2658-2 (hc) — 978-1-4222-9199-3 (ebook)

Printing (last digit) 9 8 7 6 5 4 3 2 1
Printed and bound in the United States of America.
CPSIA Compliance Information: Batch #S2013. For further information, contact Mason Crest at 1-866-MCP-Book.

About the Author: Aldo Wandersman is a journalist and publicist who has worked with some of the leading press agencies in Brazil. Since the 1980s, he has written on a variety of current issues, and has more than 1,000 articles published in the Brazilian press. He was editor of the magazine *Culture Facts* and collaborated with some of Brazil's leading newspapers, including *O Globo* and *Jornal do Brazil*. He is the author of the book *Personal Revolution in the Digital Age*, published by Editora Scortecci in 2001. The author is fond of football; he began attending the Maracana in 1965 when he was eight years old, and was among the fans who attended the last World Cup tournament in South Africa.

Photo credits: AgenciaBrasil: 7, 10, 18; EFE: 12; EFE/Alberto Estévez: 17; EFE/Ferraro: 8; EFE/DPA/Bernd Weissbrod: 23; Alexandru Cristian Ciobanu / Shutterstock.com: 2; fstockfoto / Shutterstock.com: 27 (left), 28; Eoghan McNally / Shutterstock.com: 26 (bottom); sportgraphic / Shutterstock.com: 1, 4, 14, 21, 24, 26 (top), 27 (right).

TABLE OF CONTENTS

CHAPTER 1. A Difficult Start   5

CHAPTER 2. The Arrival of "Ronaldinho"   9

CHAPTER 3. The Phenomenon Gains Glory   15

CHAPTER 4. Starting Over   19

CHAPTER 5. The Greatest Scorer
            in World Cup History   25

Further Reading / Internet Resources   31

INDEX   32

Ronaldo in action during a World Cup game. The Phenomenon, as he was known, would retire as the all-time leading scorer in World Cup history with 15 goals.

CHAPTER 1

A Difficult Start

FEW KNEW THE WAY TO THE GOAL as well as the Brazilian superstar Ronaldo Luiz Nazario de Lima. He demolished enemy defenses with amazing speed, and often only stopped when the ball was resting at the back of the net. More than any other player, Ronaldo built a myth around the jersey number 9, leaving his mark wherever he went. The striker wore the jerseys of some of the biggest clubs in Europe, at different times delighting fans of the Spanish rivals FC Barcelona and Real Madrid, and of Inter Milan in Italy. But his most enduring fame came when he was wearing the yellow and green jersey of the Brazilian national team. He led Brazil to victory at the 2002 Korea-Japan World Cup, and in 2006 established himself as the top goalscorer in World Cup history. He was also elected three times as the best player in the world. The nickname he received as a young player, "the Phenomenon," is the most appropriate name for a player as complete as Ronaldo.

Born on September 22, 1976 in Bento Ribeiro, a neighborhood in the northern part of Rio de Janeiro, Ronaldo Luiz Nazario de Lima was the youngest of three brothers from a family of modest means. From an early age he began playing with the ball on the court in the neighborhood. Eventually he joined the football team at Valqueire a modest club near his home. He went there to play when he was not in school.

It was on the small soccer field at Valqueire that Ronaldo developed his enviable ability to control the ball in tight spaces, as well as the extraordinary mental agility that would mark his career.

Next, he went to the club Ramos, where he moved quickly through the lower levels. At one point, he was offered an opportunity to train with Flamengo, one of the most important teams in Rio de Janeiro. This would have been a dream come true, as Flamengo was Ronaldo's favorite team when he was growing up. However, he could not afford to purchase a bus tickets to attend Flamengo's training camp in the remote district of Gavea. This ended the dream.

The Phenomenon Is Born

Instead, Ronaldo had to be content with playing for the junior team of Sao Cristovao. Unlike Flamengo, this smaller club in Rio did not have a tradition of great achievement in soccer. However, the club agreed to pay the cost of transporting Ronaldo to training.

His start on the soccer field of Sao Cristovao marked Ronaldo's entry into the higher levels of the game. Years later, the club would demonstrate its pride by posting an enormous sign in the stadium bleachers that read, "Here was born the Phenomenon."

At age 14, Ronaldo's soccer skills began to attract the attention of talent scouts, who looked for promising young players and tried to sign them to the larger Brazilian clubs. Two clubs, Botafogo and Sao Paulo, expressed an interest in the young player, but the negotiations fell through.

It was Jairzinho, a former star of the Brazilian national team that had won the World Cup in 1970, who helped Ronaldo move up to the highest ranks of Brazilian soccer. Jairzinho recommended the young striker to the managers of Cruzeiro Sports Club, a first division team where he had played during the 1970s. In 1993, the team paid $10,000 to bring the young striker to Minas Gerais, the Brazilian state where Cruzeiro is based.

First Appearance for Brazil

That same year, while playing for Cruzeiro's junior team, Ronaldo received his first call to wear the shirt of Brazil. He joined the Brazilian under-17 team for the 1993 South American U-17 Championship. The team had a disappointing performance, finishing fourth in the tournament and failing to qualify for the U-17 World Cup for the first time in its history. However, Ronaldo stood out as the tournament's top scorer with eight goals.

The lack of money to pay his bus fare ended Ronaldo's dream of playing with Flamengo, the favorite club of his childhood. But even playing for the modest team of Sao Cristovao, Ronaldo achieved the spotlight and earned his first call to the national team of Brazil. Beginning with the under-17 team, Ronaldo always showed that he could find the goal. He was the top scorer in the 1993 South American Championship, scoring eight times.

The former player Ronaldo Nazario during a meeting at the Brazilian Ministry of Sports speaks about issues related to the 2014 World Cup, which will be held in Brazil.

Ronaldo's success with the under-17 team led the directors of Cruzeiro to move the striker from the club's junior ranks. At age 16, Ronaldo signed his first professional contract to defend the colors of Cruzeiro. He soon had the opportunity to join the core team of Cruzeiro, and did not disappoint. In his first tournament with the club, the 1993 Brazil Cup, he scored 12 goals in 14 games, and finished among the top three scorers in the competition. He helped Cruzeiro win the Brazil Cup for the first time in the club's history.

Among the memorable performances with the shirt of Cruzeiro, the fans will never forget the three goals Ronaldo scored in a victory over rival Atletico Mineiro.

Some of his most memorable performances included a game against Bay in which Ronaldo scored five goals. When Cruzeiro played a tour in Portugal, Ronaldo left the field to a standing ovation by the Portuguese fans after scoring the only goal in a victory over Belenenses. His performances caught the attention of the European media. On returning to Brazil, Cruzeiro received its first offer from a European club. Inter Milan offered $500,000 for Ronaldo in late 1993.

The following season began with Cruzeiro seeking the state championship of Minas Gerais. Again, Ronaldo was the top player for the club, scoring 22 times and becoming the tournament's top scorer. It was clear that the teenager had an extraordinary talent with the ball at his feet.

Ronaldo celebrates a goal for Inter Milan in 1998.

CHAPTER 2

The Arrival of "Ronaldinho"

IN MARCH OF 1994, RONALDO HAD HIS FIRST OPPORTUNITY to play with the senior team of Brazil. He was summoned by coach Carlos Alberto Parreira to play a friendly match against Argentina. In May, he played for Brazil again in the team's final match before the start of the 1994 World Cup. Ronaldo scored one of Brazil's three goals in a win over Iceland, and earned a spot on the World Cup roster. This matched the accomplishment of the great Pele's, who also was 17 when he played in his first World Cup.

When he arriving on the national team, Ronaldo was still very young, slender, and seemingly fragile. He quickly received the nickname Ronaldinho ("little Ronaldo") to distinguish him from another player on the team, Ronaldo Rodrigues de Jesus. The older player, a defender from Sao Paulo, became known as Ronaldão ("big Ronaldo").

During the World Cup tournament in the United States, Ronaldo did play. He was a spectator from the bench as the Brazilian team won the Cup for the fourth time. Fans called for Ronaldo to get a chance to play, but despite their repeated requests, Coach Parreira decided to substitute other players in the final.

Even though he did not have an opportunity to participate in the games, the opportunity to practice with the major stars of Brazilian football, especially Romario, helped Ronaldo to improve his skills. That experience, plus his strength and youth, made it likely that one day Ronaldo would star for Brazil in a World Cup tournament.

In the footsteps of Romario

After the 1994 World Cup, Ronaldo was considered by much of the press as the top young player in Brazilian football. Soon after the team returned from the United States, Cruzeiro received a proposal for his services from a European club. PSV

From his seat on the bench, Ronaldo was privileged to watch the brilliant play of the Brazilian star Romario in the 1994 World Cup.

Eindhoven paid $6 million for the right to bring Ronaldo to Europe for the 1994-95 season. Ronaldo's Brazilian teammate Romario had advised the young striker to join the Dutch club. Romario had previously played six seasons at PSV.

In his first season at PSV, Ronaldo was the top scorer in the Dutch League. He scored 35 goals in 36 official games. The next year he would continue this torrid scoring pace, with 19 goals in 21 games. However, Ronaldo suffered a knee injury in late 1995 that forced him to miss about half of the season. He had surgery on his right knee in February 1996. Despite the recommendation of doctors that he should take time to recover, Ronaldo was back on the field by April of that year, in time to help PSV win the 1996 Dutch Cup.

Ronaldo began to dream of greater things. After scoring a total of 67 goals in 71 games in Holland, he knew that it was only a matter of time before the major soccer clubs of Europe came calling. After the 1995-96 season both Inter Milan and FC Barcelona attempted to acquire the player. Barcelona made the larger offer, worth about $17 million, and soon Ronaldo was wearing the Barça jersey.

A Superstar in Spain

Ronaldo's arrival in Spain for the 1996-97 season caused a sensation in the Spanish media and among fans of FC Barcelona. There were high expectations for the young striker, but he quickly justified the large investment by Barça. Ronaldo scored 34 goals in 37 Spanish League games, leading the league. He led the team to victories in the Copa del Rey and Spanish Supercup tournaments. He also helped Barcelona win the UEFA Cup Winners' Cup, a prestigious tournament that is no longer played, scoring the only goal in the 1997 final against Paris Saint-Germain.

Fans of FC Barcelona will never forget the image of Ronaldo sprinting toward the goal, breaking through defenses like a Spanish bull that can not be contained. While he was in Barcelona Ronaldo established a gesture that became his trademark—he would celebrate his goals by running with his arms outstretched like an airplane. Overall, in 49 games with Barça during 1996-97 Ronaldo scored an amazing 47 goals. There was no doubt the boy from Brazil was ready to fly even higher.

The Spanish media lavished praise on Ronaldo. There seemed to be no way to describe this 20-year-old who gave high-level performances every game other than as "the Phenomenon." His first season in Spain was an incredible display of talent and skill. From this point on, greatness would always be expected of Ronaldo.

The young striker's place in the soccer world was confirmed in late 1996, when for the first time he was elected FIFA World Player of the Year by the international media, coaches, and players. Ronaldo was the youngest player ever to receive the prestigious award.

The Best in the World

Ronaldinho enjoyed the lifestyle in Spain. He was appreciated by the local press and beloved by the Barça fans. It seemed as though Ronaldo and FC Barcelona had been made for each other. Therefore, it was a huge surprise when, at the end of his first season with FC Barcelona, the story broke that the Italian club Inter Milan had acquired his services. The club paid Barcelona a buy-out fee, and signed Ronaldo to a contract worth $32 million. At the time, it was the largest soccer contract in history.

Ronaldo was in Norway, playing a friendly match with the Brazilian national

Perhaps it was fate that the career of Ronaldo would have interesting parallels to that of Romario, one of his heroes. During the 1994 World Cup in the United States, Ronaldo watched from the bench as Romario did wonderful things in the field. After the World Cup, when PSV from Holland was looking for an up-and-coming star to replace Romario, they immediately hired Ronaldo. Then, when Romario said goodbye to FC Barcelona, the Spanish club hired the Phenomenon to replace Romario and command their attack.

In 1994, 17-year-old Ronaldo Luis Nazario De Lima was asked to join the Brazilian national team for the World Cup tournament. He is pictured in the back row, fifth from the left, in this photo of the Cup-winning national team.

team in preparation for the 1997 Copa América, when his agent informed him about the transfer to the Italian club. He was disappointed to be leaving Spain, but happy for the challenge of playing in Italy, which has one of the world's top professional soccer leagues, He looked forward to defending the colors of Inter Milan.

First, though, Ronaldo would help the Brazilian team win the Copa América, scoring five goals. One came in the tournament final against Bolivia, breaking a 1-1 tie in a game Brazil would go on to win by a 3-1 score. It was the first time that a defending World Cup champion had won the Copa América title. Ronaldo received the Golden Ball as the tournament's best player.

In 1997 Ronaldo would team up with Romario to lead Brazil to victory in the Confederations Cup. This made Brazil the first team to hold the World Cup, Confederations Cup, and the championship of their confederation (in Brazil's case, CONMEBOL) at the same time. Romario scored six goals, Ronaldo four.

To cap off a great year, at the end of 1997 Ronaldo was chosen as FIFA World Player of the Year for the second straight time.

Arrival in Italy

Before Ronaldo joined Inter Milan for the 1997-98 season, the Italian club had not won a *scudetto* (the national championship in Italy) in seven years. His first public appearnce in Milan paralyzed the city, and everything was a big celebration. His debut in the black and blue shirt of Inter Milan came in a friendly match against Manchester United, which was watched by more than 60,000 fans who sold out the Giuseppe Meazza stadium.

To this point, Ronaldo had won the number 9 shirt, but when he arrived at Inter the Chilean Ivan Zamorano had that number and was unwilling to give it up. So in his first season with the club Ronaldo wore the number 10. The phenomenon soon showed that the number on the back did not matter.

Ronaldo scored 34 goals in 47 matches, setting a record for most goals by a foreign-born player in his first season of Italy's top soccer league, Serie A. Ronaldo also improved as a player in many ways. He became a better passer, and was among the league leaders in assists. He also became more of a leader, and by the end of the season he was the team's captain.

The 1997-98 league title would elude Inter Milan. The club reached the final against Italian powerhouse Juventus. In a highly controversial play, Ronaldo seemed to have clearly been fouled. However, the official did not call the penalty and Juventus went on to win the *scudetto* that year.

It was consolation to the fans when Ronaldo led Inter Milan to victory in the 1998 UEFA Cup. He scored six goals during the tournament, including one in the 3-0 final victory over Lazio.

It had been a tremendous season, and now Ronaldo was able to turn his attention back to the Brazilian national team, which was preparing to defend its world championship in the 1998 World Cup finals.

Widely considered the best player in the world, Ronaldo expected that the 1998 World Cup would be an opportunity for great glory. But although he played very well overall, an unexpected illness before the final match led to disaster for Brazil.

CHAPTER 3

The Phenomenon Gains Glory

AS THE BRAZILIAN TEAM PREPARED TO DEFEND ITS TITLE at the 1998 World Cup finals, to be held in France, sports reporters all over the world were certain that the event would mark Ronaldo's moment of glory. As the world's best player two years in a row, there were high expectations for the Brazilian striker. These were heightened once the Brazilian coach, Mário Zagallo, left Romario off the national team's roster for the World Cup. This meant that the Phenomenon would be the biggest star on the Brazilian team. Could Ronaldo lead Brazil to an unprecedented fifth World Cup victory, or was there too much responsibility on his shoulders?

Even though Romario would not be playing, the Brazilian team still included several players who had lifted the World Cup in 1994, including the team captain, Dunga. However, there was no doubt that Ronaldo was the team's biggest star. This was evident even when the team trained, as hundreds of journalists tried to get the player's attention before, during, and after practice. Ronaldo tried to meet their demands.

The Brazilian squad was effective, easily advancing out of the group stage with victories over Morocco and Scotland. However, most observers were surprised that Ronaldo did not contribute much. In the squad's first three games, he only scored one goal, in a 3-0 win over Morocco.

Ronaldo began to heat up in the knock-out stage. In the team's first game, against Chile, he scored twice against the squad of his Inter Milan teammate Ivan Zamorano for a 4-1 Brazil victory.

In the semifinals, against the always dangerous Dutch team, Ronaldo scored Brazil's only goal in regular time. The game ended in a 1-1 tie and had to be decided with penalty kicks. Ronaldo scored his penalty, helping Brazil to once again reached the final game of the World Cup.

A Disappointing End

The coaches and fans of the Brazilian team were optimistic before the World Cup final. Most people felt that the 1998 team led by coach Zagallo was not as good as the Brazilian squad of 1970, which Zagallo had also managed. That brilliant team had included such outstanding players as Pelé, Tostão, and Jairzinho. However, Brazilians believed that in a crucial moment, the Phenomenon would make a difference.

It would not be easy for Brazil. Their opponent in the World Cup final, France, was the host country for the tournament.

The French team was led by the great striker Zinedine Zidane, and the game would be played at the Stade de France in Paris on July 12, 1998. However, Brazilian fans pointed out that "Les Bleu," the French national team, had never won the World Cup, while the yellow and green typically ended up as world champions in the end.

But unknown to most fans in this climate of high expectations, behind the scenes a major problem was developing just before the final. The night before the match, Ronaldo suffered a mysterious seizure and collapsed. Some of his teammates, who saw the fit, called the medical authorities. Ronaldo was taken to the hospital for tests.

As a result, on the morning of the final game, when Coach Zagallo released his starting roster Brazilians fans were shocked to see the name "Edmundo" among the forwards instead of "Ronaldo." Something was not right, the anxious fans told themselves. Maybe the coach had made a mistake.

Less than 90 minutes before the match, Ronaldo arrived at the locker room and

With Internazionale Milan, Ronaldo would have wear a shirt other than 9 for the first time in his career. At that time, the number belonged to to the Chilean Zamorano. Even without the number nine on the back Ronaldo had a spectacular season with the Milanese team, becoming the league's top scorer. At the end of 1997, the football world once again confirmed Ronaldo's status as the best player on the planet. All this naturally made him the star of the French Cup. But a medical issue that to this day has never been fully explained postponed for four years Ronaldo's dream of winning the World Cup.

said that he could play. The doctors did not know what had caused his fit, and the player had never had this problem before. The team was divided. Some of the Brazilian players, who had seen Ronaldo collapse, feared that he was not healthy enough to help the team. Others wanted the Phenomenon on the field. Ultimately, Coach Zagallo did not dare to leave Ronaldo out of the World Cup final. Number 9 would go onto the field with the rest of the team.

It was clear from the start that Ronaldo was not himself. He seemed slow and sluggish. (It would later turn out that the doctors had given him drugs to treat epilepsy.) About a half-hour into the game, shortly after Zidane had scored to give France a 1-0 lead, Ronaldo received a pass from Dunga in the goaltenders box but he could not convert the goal. He collided with the French goaltender, Fabien Barthez, and was knocked unconscious. Although he recovered and remained in the game, it was clear to observers that the Phenomenon would not make a difference for Brazil this time.

Ronaldo's unusual illness seemed to demoralize the entire Brazilian team. The French team won the match 3-0, and earned the right for French fans to celebrate late into the night on the streets of Paris.

Afterward, no one was exactly certain what had happened to Ronaldo on the

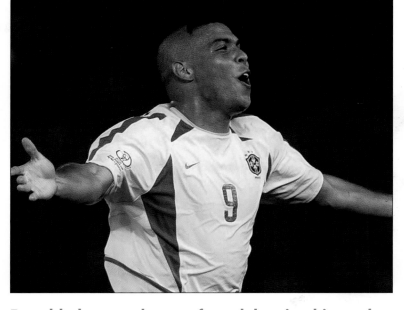

Ronaldo became known for celebrating his goals by running with his arms stretched out wide, like the wings of an airplane.

night before the final. His teammates thought he had an epileptic seizure, but others speculated that he might have had a a mild heart attack or even just a case of nerves. Some even raised the possibility that he had been poisoned or drugged by the French. The World Cup loss was so upsetting that the legislature of Brazil launched an official investigation. However, the matter has never been explained to the satisfaction of all Brazilian fans.

The French star Zidane would go on to be named FIFA World Player of the Year in 1998. Although Ronaldo was runner-up for the award, the strange circumstances of Brazil's 1998 World Cup loss would lead to questions about his physical condition on the field that could not easily be answered.

Ronaldo presents one of his jerseys to Brazilian President Luiz Inacio Lula da Silva. After the disappointment of France, and after overcoming many injuries, Ronaldo would achieve redemption by helping Brazil win the 2002 World Cup.

CHAPTER 4

Starting Over

THE 1998-99 ITALIAN SEASON BEGAN WITH RONALDO still trying to erase the bitter memory of Brazil's World Cup defeat in France. He would now wear jersey number 9 for the *nerazurri*, as Inter Milan is known. (The nickname refers to the team's black and blue uniforms.) He was in the spotlight, as the fans hoped he would help Inter finally earn the *scudetto*. Ronaldo performed well when he was on the field, scoring 14 goals—the most on the club—in just 19 games. However, the striker missed a large part of the Italian season due to a knee injury, and Inter Milan would again fall short of the championship.

When Ronaldo was summoned to play for Brazil in the 1999 Copa América, he showed that he still had plenty to contribute to the team. In the quarterfinals, he scored both goals in a victory over Argentina. He netted another in the 3-0 victory over Uruguay in the final, as Brazil hoisted the Cup once again.

When he returned to Inter Milan to contest the second round of the Italian championship, he suffered a serious injury in a match against Lecce. Ronaldo hurt his right knee and had to spend five months off the field. The injury also kept him out of the lineup for the Confederations Cup, which Mexico won over Brazil.

2000: A year to forget

Because of his success, Ronaldo was paid to represent some of the biggest

Pele created the myth around the shirt number 10. In the 2002 World Cup, Ronaldo created a similar mystique around the number 9 shirt.

brands in the world, such as the sporting goods company Nike. As a result, Ronaldo became one of the most recognizable faces in the world. However, when the player didn't perform well, some people said it was because he had too many commitments away from the field. Ronaldo lived a busy life, and was always in the eye of the paparazzi.

Ronaldo put some order to his personal life in 1999 when he married Milene Domingues. This young Brazilian soccer player was not only beautiful, she also had an uncanny ability with the ball, which led the media to call her "Ronaldinha." In April 2000, the couple's first child, a son named Ronald, was born.

By that point Ronaldo was in the final phase of rehabilitation from his knee injury. On April 12, a week after the birth of his son, Ronaldo rejoined Inter Milan for a match against Lazio. It was an important match for the Coppa Italia.

The first time Ronaldo received a pass, early in the match, he was running toward the Lazio goal. When he attempted to change direction and fool the defenders, his right knee collapsed. The Phenomenon fell to the grass screaming in pain, as cameras recorded the dramatic knee injury.

Many people thought this second knee injury would be the end of his career. Some speculated that perhaps his recovery from the original injury should have been longer, but that his sponsors had pushed for Ronaldo to return too quickly.

Ronaldo vowed to return, but his second knee injury was very serious. Doctors said it would be at least a year before Ronaldo could begin playing soccer again.

Patience and Persistence are Key to Recovery

Ronaldo spent the 2000-01 season in the same way that he had spent most of the previous year—trying to get back into condition. He was on crutches for the first few months of the injury. After he was cleared by doctors to begin working out, members of the media would report on his visits to the gym and the slow pace of his recovery.

Inter fans, as well as fans of the player, were saddened to see these images, and many thought that number 9 would never be the same player that he had once been. He missed the entire 2000-01 season. It would take 15 long months before Ronald was ready to return to the soccer field.

His return finally came in a UEFA Cup match against Brasov Romania in September 2001. Ronaldo substituted for his countryman Adriano in the 51st minute. He appeared in 16 games for Inter in the 2001-02 season, scoring seven goals. Early in the season, however, he found himself watching the action from the bench most of the time.

Ronaldo in action for Real Madrid. He signed with the club for a record 30 million Euros in 2002. The club's huge investment began to pay off immediately, as his jersey sales broke all records on the first day. During 127 appearances with the club from 2002 to 2007, Ronaldo scored a total of 83 goals. He led the Spanish League in scoring for the 2003-04 season, winning the Pichichi Trophy.

For Inter Milan, things seemed to be changing for the better in early 2002. Even without Ronaldo at his best, the club was leading the Italian League late in the season. The club seemed to have a lock on the title that had eluded it for more than a dozen years.

The Serie A final would be played against Lazio, the club that had started Ronaldo's nightmare. It seemed like the perfect opportunity for Ronaldo to show that he was fully recovered, and to lift the coveted *scudetto* for the first time with Inter Milan.

Ronaldo started the game, and Inter jumped out to a 2-1 lead. However, the team collapsed in the second half. Ronaldo was removed from the game, but even that could not help the club. Lazio won the title by a 4-2 score. Afterward, the cameras captured Ronaldo weeping. As he left the field the Brazilian striker told reporters, "Disappointment is my companion." Definitely, the football gods seemed to have deserted him.

The Return of the Brazilian

Brazilian fans were concerned when national team coach Luiz Felipe Scolari included Ronaldo's name on the list of players who would go to Asia to play for the 2002 World Cup. No one was certain that the player was over his injuries, or that he wouldn't get hurt again. When he joined the Brazilian team Ronaldo had a huge scar on his right knee. In his first few games he seemed completely out of rhythm because

of the extended period in which he had been inactive.

Many in Brazil wanted to see Romario, star of the 1994 World Cup, back in the lineup for the yellow and green instead of Ronaldo. Romario had been left off the team in 1998 because of an injury. Although he was 36 years old, he was still one of the top players in Brazil, and fans thought he might be able to drive the Brazilian attack.

However, Coach Scolari, a strong personality, ignored criticism from the press. He was convinced that Brazil should have Ronaldo on the attack. Ronaldo wore the green and yellow jersey in a March 2002 friendly against Yugoslavia. He played again for Brazil in May against Malaysia, scoring a goal. This performance revived hopes that Ronaldo could help Brazil in its quest for the fifth World Cup title.

World Cup Redemption

Ronaldo's performance at the 2002 World Cup, which was jointly hosted by Korea and Japan, surpassed even the most optimistic forecasts. He was the tournament's top scorer with eight goals, and recorded a goal in every game except Brazil's quarterfinal win over England. With teamates Rivaldo (five goals) and Ronaldinho Gaúcho (two goals), Brazil had an unstoppable attack. The team easily won its three games in the group stage, then defeated Belgium and England to reach the semifinals. Ronaldo then scored the only goal in against Turkey to take Brazil to the final.

Against Germany, Ronaldo scored his seventh and eighth goals of the tournament as Brazil won its fifth World Cup title by a score of 2-0.

Ronaldo's inspired performance at the highest level of soccer stunned the world. He was hailed as a hero in Brazil, although the player was modest afterward. "In both good times and difficult times, we must have patience," he said. "Things happen as they should. I am very happy with my performance, with two goals in the final and the victory of Brazil. Now I just want to celebrate."

The Phenomenon had returned and had every reason to celebrate. His tremendous performance had erased from memory the disastrous World Cup loss in France four years earlier. At the end of the 2002 season, Ronaldo was chosen for a third time as the FIFA World Player of the Year. He was the first player ever to win the award three times, although later Zidane and the Argentine Lionel Messi would match his accomplishment. Ronaldo proved that he had returned to the top of international soccer.

Ronaldo celebrates after scoring one of his two goals in the World Cup final against Germany.

When looking at the career of Ronaldo in the years before the 2002 World Cup, an observer must take into account the number of very serious injuries he suffered. The cameras of the world recorded the moment that he suffered serious damage to the tendons of his right knee. He spent nearly two years away from the soccer field as he tried to make a slow and difficult recovery. Despite all of the work that he put in to getting healthy, even the most optimistic Brazilian fans couldn't imagine the memorable performance put on by the Phenomenon in leading Brazil to win its fifth World Cup in 2002.

Ronaldo in action with Real Madrid, 2004.

CHAPTER 5

The Greatest Scorer in World Cup History

After his revival in the 2002 World Cup, Ronaldo was again a priority for the big European clubs. At first, he wanted to return to FC Barcelona, but the club from Spain was experiencing financial troubles that prevented it from making a good offer to Ronaldo. Instead, the striker received an offer of 30 million Eurps to wear the shirt of Barcelona's biggest rival, Real Madrid. The move made Ronaldo part of a small group of players who had defended the colors of the top two teams in Spain.

Real Madrid Dream Team

Real Madrid brought Ronaldo aboard in part because of his great showing at the Asian World Cup, but there was also a strong marketing component to the decision. The idea of the merengue club was to assemble a cast of all-star players—called "galácticos" in the media—to create a team that, on paper at least, would be unbeatable. Toward this goal the club had already hired Luis Figo, a former teammate of Ronaldo at Barcelona, in 2000, and the French star Zinedine Zidane, in 2001. After Ronaldo joined the club in 2002, other major stars included the striker's fellow Brazilian, Roberto Carlos, and in 2003 the English midfielder David Beckham.

This constellation of stars was undoubtedly a team to be admired. Even its training sessions were watched by thousands of fanatical fans. Real Madrid used its star players to sell tickets and merchandise around the world.

Ronaldo played with his friend Roberto Carlos at Real Madrid from 2002 to 2007.

For example, Ronaldo's jersey broke records for shirt sales after he signed in 2002. The sale of merchandise helped to increase the club's fan base, and its value, greatly. By 2006 Real Madrid was the most valuable soccer club in the world thanks to the fame of its *galácticos* and the resources they generated.

Ronaldo's performance was uneven. A minor injury left him unable to play for the club until October 2002, but the fans kept on chanting his name. In his first game, the striker scored twice in a 4-2 rout over Alavés. Ronaldo was overweight and not in great condition. He was taken out for substitutes in 22 of the 35 matches he played for Real Madrid in the 2002-03 season. Still, he scored 23 goals, placing him among the league leaders. His scoring helped the club win the Spanish League championship in 2003. His final goal of the season came in the last game, against Athletic Bilbao. Oddly enough, the coveted Spanish League title was the first regional tournament won by the Phenomenon in his professional career.

With Real Madrid, Ronaldo also won an Intercontinental Cup in 2002 and the in 2003.

In the years that followed, the *galacticos* of Real Madrid received more media attention than they deserved due to their play. The team started the 2003-04 season well, wining the Spanish Supercup and leading the league until late. They sometimes received magnificent play from Ronaldo, Zidane, and

There was a certain magic to see the constellation of super-stars in the field wearing the Real Madrid jerseys. The team boasted many of the biggest names in international soccer. At the time they played together with Real Madrid, Ronaldo and his French teammate Zinedine Zidane were the only two players in history to win the "best player" title from FIFA three times. They have since been joined in that accomplishment by the Argentine star Lionel Messi.

During the 2006 World Cup Ronaldo was expected to support younger players like Adriano and Ronaldinho Gaúcho.

the newcomer Beckham. Ronaldo scored 24 goals, the most in the Spanish League. However, Real Madrid lost its last five matches and finished fourth in La Liga. The club also lost in the finals of the Copa del Rey to Real Zaragoza, and was eliminated from the UEFA Champions League.

The 2004-05 and 2005-06 seasons were also disappointing. Both years, Ronaldo led the team in goals. He scored 21 goals in 2004-05 and 14 goals in 2005-06. However, in both seasons Real Madrid finished second in the Spanish League to its rival FC Barcelona.

World Cup 2006

Even though Ronaldo was not the same player that he had been when he was younger, he was still one of the best players

in the world in 2006. After all, in 127 matches with Real Madrid he had scored 83 goals. It was therefore natural that Carlos Alberto Parreira, coach of the Brazilian national team, would call his name in preparation for the 2006 World Cup.

When Ronaldo began the campaign for Brazil's sixth victory at the World Cup in Germany, he would not be the star of the team. However, he was an important component of the "magic square" formed by Kaka, Adriano, and Ronaldinho.

Even though the team contained some of the best players in world soccer, the Brazilians had a disappointing tournament. They won all three games in the group stage and advanced to the knockout stage. Ronaldo contributed two goals in the

Ronaldo battles Dario Simic of Croatia for the ball during the 2006 World Cup. Although during the game fans criticized Ronaldo for being overweight and slow, he went on to set the World Cup finals scoring record.

match against Japan. He scored his third goal of the tournament in the team's knock-out stage win over Ghana. This earned Brazil a World Cup rematch against France and Zidane. However, the dream of a sixth title ended with a 1-0 loss to the French.

While the World Cup in Germany did not allow Brazil to add another star to their

> Gerd Müller declared that he was happy that Ronaldo had gained the record, after the Brazilian overtook him as the leading goalscorer of the World Cup.

national team's shirt, Ronaldo at least achieved a remarkable record. With the three goals he scored, he became the leading scorer in in the history of the World Cup, a total of 15 goals in four appearances. This surpassed the previous record of 14 goals, by the German Gerd Müller, which had been set more than 30 years earlier.

The World Cup final in Germany marked the end of Ronaldo's career with the Brazilian national team. The partnership had produced two World Cup titles (1994 and 2002), a second-place finish (1998), and his place as the tournament's top goal-scorer.

The Return to Milan

Despite the failure of the Brazil in the German World Cup, Ronaldo showed that he could still play at a high level. During the 2006-07 season he was not getting as much playing time at Real Madrid, so he negotiated a return to Milan, Italy. This time, however, he would play for AC Milan, the archrival of his former club Internazionale. Thus Ronaldo became one of the few players to wear the shirt of both of the two main Italian teams.

At AC Milan, Ronaldo joined two distinguished Brazilians, Kaka and Alexandre Pato. They formed an attacking trio that the Italian press dubbed "Ka-Pa-Ro."

Wearing the number 99 shirt, as the number nine was already assigned, Ronaldo played in six matches with AC Milan. He scored two goals and an assist in a victory over Siena. Milan finished only fifth in Serie A. Although the club did win the UEFA Super Cup in 2007, Ronaldo was not allow to play because of his transfer from Real Madrid. He had to watch as his teammates lifted the trophy.

The 2007-08 season started with promise for Ronaldo. In a January match against Napoli, he scored twice while Kaka and Pato also gave an excellent performance. Fans of AC Milan hoped this would be a year of great celebrations. Then the Phenomenon's worst nightmare occurred. In a February match against Livorno, Ronaldo suffered another knee injury. This ended his season, and also his time in Italian soccer. Because of the injury, AC Milan was unwilling to renew the player's contract for the next year.

The Move to Corinthians

After leaving Italy, Ronaldo returned to Rio de Janeiro and went through a long period of recovery. He worked out in the facilities at Flamengo, the favorite club of his childhood. Many people thought that Ronaldo would put on the red-and-black shirt of Flamengo when he was able to return to the field. To general surprise, however, he ended up signing a contract with Corinthians. He was introduced to fans of the club at a big party in December 2008. Fourteen years after leaving Brazil, Ronaldo had returned.

Because his knee had been so badly injured, Ronaldo's recovery was slow. His first goal for Corinthians came in a March 2009 game against the club's rival, Palmeiras. He played a key role in the Corinthians victory in the state championship, scoring 20 goals in 30 matches. He also helped Corinthians win the Brazil Cup, which qualified the team to participate in the 2010 Copa Libertadores.

However, the 2010 Copa Libertadores was a disappointment. Corinthians earned the first seed after its performance in the group stage, but lost in the first round of the knockout stage to Flamengo despite a goal in the second leg by Ronaldo.

In 2010 Corinthians finished the Brazilian championship in third place. Ronaldo scored nine goals in 20 games and helped the club qualify for the 2011 Copa

Libertadores. Once again, however, Corinthians exited the tournament early, this time losing in the first round to Deportes Tolima.

Farewell to the Game

After the 2011 Copa Libertadores loss, Ronaldo realized that it was time to end his professional career. On February 14, 2011, he held a press conference to officially announce his retirement from the game. "After one more injury, I thought a lot at home and decided it was time," said a visibly moved Ronaldo. "I can not play any longer. I have given all that I could. It is very hard to abandon what makes you happy—you have so much love and could continue because mentally and psychologically you still want a lot. But I have also taken some losses. I have lost to my body."

The announcement of Ronaldo's retirement made headlines around the world. The official website of FIFA stamped the phrase "Always a Phenomenon" on a story about the farewell of the highest scorer in the history of the World Cup. In France, the newspaper *L'Equipe* showed a picture of Ronaldo with the FIFA World Cup 2002

and said that the Corinthians press room was so crowded with journalists that they could not all fit inside the room. The *Daily Mail* of England called the phenomenon a "Brazilian legend" and noted that Ronaldo cried a lot when he announced his retirement. But perhaps the best headline came from Argentina: "The goal is sad," wrote the newspaper *Olé*.

A new role in football

Away from the pitch, Ronaldo began to devote himself to his successful career as an entrepreneur in the field of sports, working in the career management of athletes from various fields, including football, wrestling and athletics.

As Brazil prepares to host the 2014 World Cup, Ronaldo accepted the invitation for the role of "Cup ambassador," a position similar to that occupied by Franz Beckenbauer, who helped Germany host the World Cup in 2006, and by Michel Platini before the 1998 French World Cup. As a result, the Phenomenon will be the face of the World Cup in Brazil in 2014. It is a fitting homage to one of the greatest players of all time.

FURTHER READING

Bueno, Eduardo. Football: The *Passion of Brazil*. New York: Leya, 2011.

Geringher, Max. *Almanac of the World Cup*. São Paulo: Editora Globo, 2010.

Leite, Milton. *The Top 11 Brazilian Players*. São Paulo: Editora Contexto, 2010.

Máximo, João, and Marcos De Castro. *The Brazilian Football Giants*. New York: Brazilian Civilization, 2011.

Nassar, Luciano Ubiraja. *The Best Football Players of Brazil*. New York: Expression and Art Publishing House, 2010.

INTERNET RESOURCES

www.istoedinheiro.com.br

Site of a major business and news magazine from Brazil.

www.veja.com.br

Site of the principal sports publication in Brasil.

http://esporte.uol.com.br/futebol/biografias/511/ronaldo/

Site of a major sports television channel in Brazil.

www.fifa.com

Official web site of the Fédération Internationale de Football Association (FIFA), the international governing body of futbol (soccer).

INDEX

1997 South American U-17 Championship, 6

AC Milan, 29
Adriano, 20, 27
Argentina, 9, 19
Atlético Mineiro, 7

Barthez, Fabien, 17
Beckham, David, 25, 26
Belgium, 22
Bolivia, 12
Brazil Cup, 7, 29

Carlos, Roberto, 25, 26
Confederations Cup, 12, 19
Copa América, 12, 19
Copa Libertadores, 29, 30
Copa del Rey, 11, 27
Coppa Italia, 20
Corinthians, 29–30
Cruzeiro, 6, 7, 10

Domingues, Milene, 20
Dutch Cup, 10
Dunga, 15, 17

Edmundo, 16
England, 22

FC Barcelona, 5, 10–11, 25
FIFA World Player of the Year award, 11, 13,
    17, 23
Figo, Luis, 25
Flamengo, 6, 29
France, 16–17, 18, 19, 23, 28

Germany, 23, 27
Ghana, 28

Inter Milan, 7, 8, 10, 11, 12, 13, 16, 19, 20

Jairzinho, 6, 16
Juventus, 13

Kaka, 27, 29

Lazio, 13, 20, 22
Livorno, 29
Lula da Silva, Luiz Inácio, 18

Manchester United, 13
Messi, Lionel, 23, 26
Mexico, 19
Müller, Gerd, 28

Paris Saint-Germain FC, 11
Parreira, Carlos Alberto, 9, 27
Pato, Alexandre, 29
Pelé, 16
PSV Eindhoven, 10, 11

Ramos, 6
Real Madrid, 5, 21, 24, 25–27, 29
Real Zaragoza, 27
Rio de Janeiro, 5, 6, 29
Rivaldo, 22
Romario, 10, 11, 12, 15, 22
Ronaldão, 9
Ronaldinho Gaúcho, 22, 27
Ronaldo Luiz Nazario de Lima
    birth and childhood of, 5–7
    with national team, 4, 5, 9–10, 12, 14,
        15–17, 18, 22–23, 27–28
    profesional career of, 4, 7, 8, 10–11,
        12–13, 19–22, 24, 25–27, 29–30

Sao Cristovao, 6
Scolari, Luiz Felipe, 22
Spanish League, 21
Spanish Supercup, 11

Tostão, 16
Turkey, 22

UEFA Cup, 13, 20
UEFA Cup Winners Cup, 11
United States, 9, 10, 11
Uruguay, 19

Valqueire, 5

World Cup, 5, 6, 7, 9–10, 11, 12, 13, 14,
    15–17, 18, 19, 22–23, 25, 27–28, 30

Zagallo, Mário, 15, 16, 17
Zamorano, Ivan, 13, 16
Zidane, Zinedine, 16, 17, 23, 25, 26, 28